PIGS ARE PERFECT

Also by Celia Haddon

FAITHFUL TO THE END:
THE *DAILY TELEGRAPH* ANTHOLOGY OF DOGS

THE LOVE OF CATS:
THE *DAILY TELEGRAPH* ANTHOLOGY OF CATS

MISCHIEF AND DELIGHT:
AN ILLUSTRATED ANTHOLOGY OF KITTENS: (*with Jess McAree*)

A CHRISTMAS GARLAND

A LOVER'S POSY

A MOTHER'S POSY

THE YEARBOOK OF HOPE AND INSPIRATION

THE YEARBOOK OF COMFORT AND JOY

THE YEARBOOK OF COURAGE AND SERENITY

THE YEARBOOK OF LOVE AND WISDOM

PIGS ARE PERFECT

An Illustrated Anthology

CELIA HADDON

HEADLINE

First published in 1996
by HEADLINE BOOK PUBLISHING
10 9 8 7 6 5 4 3 2 1

British Library Cataloguing in Publication Data
Haddon, Celia
Pigs are Perfect: An Illustrated Anthology
1. Swine – Literary collections
I. Title
820. 8 ′ 036
ISBN 0 7472 1641 X

Design and computer page make up by Penny Mills
Printed and bound in Italy by Canale and C. Spa

HEADLINE BOOK PUBLISHING
A division of Hodder Headline PLC
338 Euston Road
London NW1 3BH

To the 'plum pudding' pig, the Oxford Sandy and Black.

This beautiful animal, with its golden hair and black markings, is Britain's rarest native breed. If you would like to know more about this glamorous breed, you can contact the Oxford sandy and black pig society, by writing to me c/o the publishers of this book.

Author's Note

Pigs need the society of other pigs, good food, sunshine and shade, space to roam and rootle, and a warm shelter with plenty of straw to sleep in. Help charities like the Royal Society for the Prevention of Cruelty to Animals to campaign for better conditions on farms and for better regulations about the transport of live animals. Do not buy intensively reared pork. Buy pork with the RSPCA Freedom food label, or pork from pigs that have been kept in humane conditions.

CONTENTS

PIGS IN ANCIENT AND MODERN HISTORY

Pigs, nowadays locked up everywhere in sties and pens, were once born free in the woodlands. Magnificent wild boars would spend their days crunching up roots and acorns, while mother sows lovingly tended and protected their young piglets.

Man took them away from the happy forest to the restrictions of the farm, and, as the centuries progressed, enslaved them further. He locked them up for life in the filth of a smelly sty, or, worse, in the barren concrete hell of a modern factory farm.

The ancient Greeks held the pig in high esteem. Swine were sacred to the goddess Demeter, a somewhat ambiguous honour since it meant they were sacrificed to her. Homer wrote about them. Aristotle studied their love lives and their behaviour. It was in Egypt, alas, that these harmless animals became associated with the God of Evil, Set. This link may explain why Jews (and later Moslems) regarded them as unclean. But the disgrace of being unclean at least protected them from butchery in these countries.

It was the Romans who first showed that human greed could easily outdo porcine appetite. Romans were seriously greedy. They invented an amazing dish called *porcus trojanus*, which consisted of a whole pig stuffed with thrushes, larks, oysters and even nightingales. The animals were not only fattened but sometimes also tortured to death, under the mistaken idea that their flesh would thus be made more tender.

The collapse of the Roman empire brought relief to the pig. In medieval manuscripts and carvings we see a smaller, fitter and probably happier pig, allowed to roam in companionable herds in the woods or wander round the town streets. But the agricultural revolution of the eighteenth century began to put an end to pigs' freedom to root at large, while the public health reformers of the time drove them off the streets. Among the peasantry, however, the pig's lot could still be a happy one. It was the pig that protected the farm worker in Ireland from utter destitution, and could make an English worker relatively prosperous. And to keep this pig in good condition, it would often be led out of its sty to graze on the side of the roads.

In America, land of the free for pigs, they could still be found in almost every city street in the nineteenth century. Mrs Fanny Trollope, mother of the novelist Anthony, complained: 'I'm sure I should have liked Cincinnati much better if the people had not dealt so very largely in hogs! ... If I determined upon a walk up Main St, the chances were five hundred to one against my reaching the shady side without brushing by a snout or two'.

Aristotle's Notes on the Pig

Aristotle, pupil of Plato and tutor of Alexander the Great, found time to study zoology as well as philosophy. I'm afraid that he fell for some unlikely stories – that the weasel eats the herb rue before it attacks a snake, or that a female deer can be lured by music into captivity. On pigs he is rather more reliable.

The hog eats roots more than other animals, because its snout is well adapted for this operation, it is more adapted to various kinds of food than other animals. In proportion to its size its fat is developed very fast, for it becomes fat in sixty days …

These creatures are fattened with barley, millet, figs, acorns, wild pears and cucumbers. Both this and other animals with a warm stomach are fattened in idleness, and the sow also, by wallowing in the mire … The fruit of the mulberry is good for them, and abundant washings with warm water …

Vetches and figs are useful both for fattening and rearing pigs; and on the whole their food should not be all of one sort, but varied; for swine, like other animals, derive advantage from a change in their food … acorns are good for their food, but make their flesh watery.

Pig Tales from Pliny

Pliny, a Roman cavalry commander turned writer and politician, perished in the volcanic eruption of Mount Vesuvius. His book on natural history was full of delightful though unreliable stories. Later writers were so charmed by them that they repeated them for the next one and a half thousand years! Pliny's *Natural History* was translated four hundred years ago by Philemon Holland, an English doctor who had a splendid way of putting things. The eccentric spelling adds to its charm.

This is known for a truth, that when certaine theeves had tolne and driven away a companie of them [swine], the swinheard having followed them to the water side (for by that time were the theeves imbarged with them) cried aloud unto the swine, as his manner was; whereupon they knowing his voice, leaned all to one side of the vessel, turned it over and sunke it, tooke the water, and so swam againe to land unto their keeper. Moreover the hogs that use to lead and goe before the heard, are so well trained, that they wil of themselves goe to the swine-market place within the citie, and from thence home againe to their maisters, without any guid to direct them.

The Importance of Pigs

A Tudor lawyer and judge, Sir Anthony Fitzherbert wrote a treatise on farming called *The Boke of Husbandry*. In it, he included advice about farming and spiritual notes on such topics as 'A mean to put away idle thoughts in praying.' There are some words on pigs. In those days, castrated pigs were called hogs; Sir Anthony thought the practice of castration was a waste of time.

Now thou husband, that hast both horses and mares, beasts and sheep: it were necessary also, that thou have both swine and bees; for it is an old saying: he that hath both sheep, swine and bees, sleep he, wake he, he may thrive. And that saying is, because that they be those things that most profit riseth of in the shortest space, with the least cost … If thou be able to rear six pigs a year, then let two of them be boars, and four of them sows, and so to continue after the rate. For a boar will have as little keeping as a hog, and is much better than a hog, and more meat on him and is ready at all times to eat in the winter season, and to be laid in souse. And if thy sow hath more pigs than thou wilt rear, sell them, or eat them, and reare those pigs that come about Lenten time, specially the beginning of summer, for they cannot be reared in winter, for cold, without great cost.

A Calendar of Pig Care

Thomas Tusser was an Elizabethan writer who was better at telling others what to do than at doing it himself. He was an unsuccessful farmer (he probably died in a debtors' gaol) but a very successful poet. His book, *A Hundred Points of Good Husbandry*, was published in 1557 and republished throughout the sixteenth century. In his day, pigs were raised in summer, fattened through the year, and killed before winter. They ran about quite freely; the rings in their nose stopped them rooting too much. Piglets that suck on the front teats are stronger than the rest of the litter.

January
Sows ready to farrow this time of the year,
Are for to be made of, and counted full dear.
For now is the loss of a fare of the sow
More great than the loss of two calves of thy cow.

Of one sow, together, rear few above five,
And those of the fairest, and likest
    to thrive.
Ungelt, of the best keep a
    couple for store,
One boar pig and sow pig,
    that sucketh before.

September
At Michaelmas, safely, go stye up thy boar,
Lest straying abroade, ye do see him no more:
The sooner the better for Hallontide night,
The better he brawneth, if hard he do lie.

Shift boar (for ill air) as best ye do think,
And twice a day, give him fresh vittle and drink;
And diligent Cisley, my dairy good wench,
Make cleanly his cabin, for measling and stench.

To gather some mast, it shall stand thee upon,
With servant and children, ere mast be all gone:
Some left among bushes shall pleasure thy swine;
For fear of a mischief, keep acorns fro' kine.

For rooting of pasture, ring hog ye had need,
Which being well ringled, the better do feed.
Though young with their elders will lightly keep best,
Yet spare not to ringle both great and the rest.

[15]

Pigs Take a Swig

In the eighteenth century, some pigs were still allowed to roam about the farmyard. Parson James Woodforde, a country vicar in Norfolk, did some farming as well as preaching. He made his own beer and doctored his animals himself. His pigs cannot have been confined in a sty all the time, since they managed to get at one of his beer barrels.

April 15, 1778
We breakfasted, dined, supped and slept again at home. Brewed a vessell of strong Beer today. My two large Piggs, by drinking some Beer grounds taking out of one of my Barrels today, got so amazingly drunk by it, that they were not able to stand and appeared like dead things almost, and so remained all night from dinner time today. I never saw Piggs so drunk in my life, I slit their ears for them without feeling.

April 16, 1778
We breakfasted, dined, supped and slept again at home. My 2 Piggs are still unable to walk yet, but they are better than they were yesterday. They tumble about the yard and can by no means stand at all steady yet. In the afternoon my 2 Piggs were tolerably sober.

Pigs and American Freedom

The pig became a symbol of freedom to some Americans after the American War of Independence. In the British Library, I found this pamphlet, titled *The Hog, composed by a father for his son*. It was published in Washington, printed by James Wilson in 1823 and it is a charming defence of pigs.

When nature created and endowed the Hog with qualities surpassing and rare, she seems to have presented him to the statesman, lawyer, judge, physician and divine – to all the human race – as the perpetual model of that stubborn, rude, uncourtly integrity, commonly understood by the name of Independence ... Courtiers and sycophants too will flatter but neither adulation nor money can tempt him to deviate from the invariable laws of his nature, the 'even tenor of his ways', this valuable quadruped, who, though like a candidate for public office, he will go through thick and thin to reach his object, will never be led or driven like a time serving radical. The downy bed has no enchantments for him. With the Doric simplicity of a backwoodsman, he lays himself down in the humblest hovel or under 'the blue spangled arch of Heaven' and snores away the night with a full stomach and a clear conscience … The incorruptible Hog with Roman simplicity ploughs his own fields and caters for himself. Truffles and mushrooms are his choicest dainties; for his heaven, like that of the Gods, who in the reign of Saturn fought and ate with men and held sweet converse with the women, is upon the earth. There he grunts and grumbles for his competency, which, like the fund of South American riches, is concealed partly under ground, as if the deity had foreseen that tyranny would enslave, or cowardice surrender everything above its surface. But all the devices of despotism and its inquisition will not coerce him, like the Indian of the Mita, to dig dross for a master.

All hail! ye celebrated race! Since your tusky sires tore in pieces the devoted and delicate Adonis, Kings have hunted ye, and Priests have proscribed ye, as dangerous and unholy; while pensioned orators and slaves of despotic governments have attempted to ridicule a free, democratic people, by styling them the Swinish Multitude, alike invincible by military power, as the power of superstition.

New-Yorker Porkers

Charles Dickens' *American Notes*, published after a trip across the Atlantic, is full of snide comments. But he did justice to the freedom and independence of American pigs.

> Once more in Broadway! … Take care of the pigs. Two portly sows are trotting up behind this carriage, and a select party of half a dozen gentleman hogs have just now turned the corner.
>
> Here is a solitary swine lounging homewards by himself … He leads a roving, gentlemanly, vagabond kind of life, somewhat answering of that of our club-men at home. He leaves his lodging every morning at a certain hour, throws himself upon the town, gets through his day in some manner quite satisfactory to himself, and regularly appears at the door of his own house again at night. He is a free-and-easy, careless, indifferent kind of pig, having a very large acquaintance among other pigs of the same character, whom he rather knows by sight than conversation, as he seldom troubles himself to stop and exchange civilities, but goes grunting down the kennel, turning up the news and small-talk of the city in the shape of cabbage-stalks and offal … He is in every respect a republican pig, going wherever he pleases and mingling with the best society, on an equal if not superior footing, for every one makes way when he appears, and the haughtiest give him the wall if he prefer it.

By kind permission of Iona Antiques, London

THE GOLDEN AGE – FAT, FATTER, FATTEST

The golden age of the fat, indeed the positively gross pig began just before the French revolution and lasted till the beginning of the First World War. In Britain, farming became fashionable and country gentlemen started taking almost as much interest in pigs as in horses and hounds. So the pigs blossomed and grew fat, then fatter, and then fatter still.

The original old English pig, indeed the pig found throughout most of Northern Europe, had been a rangy beast, slim, slow-growing and of an independent character. In Ireland, it was called the greyhound pig, because of its long legs and muscular hams. These latter meant it could jump like a pony, but was extremely tough to eat.

New blood – from small white Chinese pigs with drooping bellies and from black, rather delicate Neapolitan pigs – transformed the British pig into a fast-maturing animal, with a remarkable capacity to put on weight.

'A good pig should have the shoulders of a parlourmaid and the buttocks of a cook,' was the maxim followed by aristocratic breeders. At agricultural shows, there was keen competition between neighbouring landowners to produce the fattest animal. Prince Albert, husband of Queen Victoria, regularly showed his huge beasts at Smithfield show in London.

Lord Hartington, later the eighth Duke of Devonshire nicknamed Harty-Tarty, was in the House of Lords one day when he heard a fellow peer pompously conclude his speech with 'This is the proudest moment of my life.'

Lord Hartington, who had three times turned down the job of prime minister, turned to his neighbour and murmured, 'The proudest moment of my life was when my pig won the first prize at Skipton Fair!'

The new porcine aristocrats were, like their owners' favourite horses and hounds, given charming and evocative names – Omega, Esau (probably because of a love of pottage!), Sobersides, Sylph, Prince Leopold, Snowflake, Lady Dolly, King Koffee, Jumbo, Beauty and Samson.

One famous breed owed its shape to a man of humble origins. The Yorkshire pig, ancestor of today's Large White and the Chester White, was bred by Joseph Tuley, a weaver in Yorkshire. He sold his pigs for such high prices that he built a Gothic cottage which he named Matchless House, after his famous sow, Matchless.

The glorious variety of modern pig breeds in Britain and America developed around the end of the last century: the black and white Berkshire, with its pricked ears, and its American cousin the Poland-China, with floppy ears; the red British Tamworth and American Duroc-Jersey; the golden spotted Oxford Sandy and Black, known as the 'plum pudding pig', the pearly Large Whites and Chester Whites, and the extraordinary Mule-footed Hog, with its uncloven trotters.

This golden age of beauty and size could not, and did not, last. Noblemen deserted the show ring and there was a new fashion for lean meat. Today, some of the old fat breeds are extinct and others are as endangered as the rhino or the whale. Only a proper conservation programme can preserve their beauty for future generations.

A Reminder to Humans

'Now look at those pigs as they lie in the straw,'
Said Dick to his father one day;
'They keep eating longer than I ever saw,
What nasty fat gluttons are they.'

'I see they are feasting,' his father replied,
'They eat a great deal, I allow;
But let us remember, before we deride,
'Tis the nature, my dear, of a sow.

'But when a great boy, such as you, my dear Dick,
Does nothing but eat all the day,
And keeps sucking good things till he makes himself sick,
What a glutton! Indeed, we may say.

'When plumcake and sugar for ever he picks,
And sweetmeats, and comfits, and figs;
Pray let him get rid of his own nasty tricks,
And then he may laugh at the pigs.'

JANE TAYLOR, *Original Poems for Infant Minds*, 1804

The Old Irish Greyhound Pig

These are tall, long-legged, bony, heavy-eared, coarse-haired animals, their throats furnished with pendulous wattles ... These swine are remarkably active, and will clear a five-barred gate as well as any hunter; on this account they should, if it be desirable to keep them, be kept in well-fenced enclosures.

When the people could keep these animals, they found them very profitable stock. The hog was indeed regarded by the Irish peasant with a peculiar degree of affection and kindness; he shared with his owner not merely the shelter of his cabin and the provisions of the children, but the warmest place at the fireside. 'The pig, the cratur' was second in importance and consideration to no inmate of the tenement he honoured with his presence, and richly too he merited the high degree of estimation in which he was held, for he did that which in many cases his poverty-ground proprietor could not have done without his aid – he paid the rent.

H. D. RICHARDSON, *Domestic Pigs, Their Origins and Varieties*, 1852

The New Fat Pigs

The wood engraver, Thomas Bewick, illustrated the new improved pig in his *History of Quadrupeds*, published in 1790. The old-fashioned common boar has tough muscular legs, while the new ones have shorter legs, showing the influence of Chinese blood. He describes an early fat pig weighing 1,215 pounds.

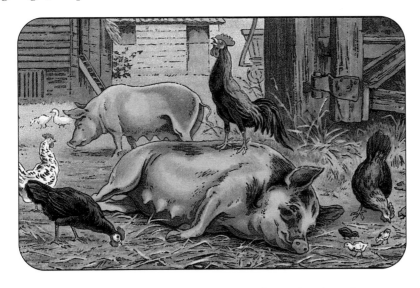

The most numerous breed of Hogs in this island is that generally known by the name of the Berkshire Pigs, now spread through almost every part of England, and some parts of Scotland ... Some of these have been fed to almost an incredible size. Mr Culley in his *Treatise on Live Stock*, gives an account of one that was killed at Congleton, in Cheshire, which measured, from the nose to the end of the tail, three yards eight inches; in height it was four feet and a half; and weighed, after it was killed, eighty-six stones eleven pounds avoirdupois.

Stately Piggeries

Nineteenth-century enthusiasts vied with each other in the splendour of their piggeries. The piggery built by Lord Moreton, at Tortworth Court, contained thirty sties, while in Minnesota a Mr Cohoon built a piggery with 'nest beds arranged directly under the large windows to give the little pigs the advantage of the early sun'. The most magnificent piggery of all was built by a Squire Barry for his Yorkshire White pigs.

The Grecian Temple for pigs at Fyling Hall, near Robin Hood's Bay in North Yorkshire, is the most splendidly appointed animal house of all. The portico and pillars are of wood, the base stone, brought by horse-drawn sledge from a local quarry half a mile away. It was built, c. 1883 by Squire Barry of Fyling Hall, an inveterate traveller who was constantly returning from abroad with some new plant, tree or architectural plan. Just such an enthusiasm was the temple, with its pillars, portico, tapering Egyptian windows, fluted frieze and acanthus-leaf drainpipe head all being concocted for pigs.

Three men took two years to build the sty. In 1948 Matthew Hart, a stonemason from Scunthorpe, recalled the frustrations of Squire Barry's incessant changes of mind as to what the style should be.

LUCINDA LAMBTON

Aristocratic Prize Pigs

The best portrait of an upper-class prize pig is to be found in P.G. Wodehouse's account of the Empress of Blandings. A Berkshire sow, she is the pride and joy of her owner, Lord Emsworth. Many are the trials and tribulations he experiences at his home, Blandings Castle, as he tries to get her into peak condition – that is, grossly fat. The most moving moment in the novel *Blandings Castle* occurs when, after a long period of being off her food, the Empress starts to eat again. Her recovery happens when she hears the proper hog call to food.

'Pig-HOOOOO-OOO-OOO-O-O-ey!' …

Slowly, fading off across the hill and dale, the vast bellow died away. And suddenly, as it died, another, softer sound succeeded it. A sort of gulpy, gurgly, plobby, squishy, wofflesome sound, like a thousand eager men drinking soup in a foreign restaurant. And, as he heard it, Lord Emsworth uttered a cry of rapture.

The Empress was feeding.

Workers' Prize Pigs

Temperance reformers and aristocratic landlords both favoured pigs – they kept workers away from the pub or from poaching. 'The grunting of a hog in a cottager's sty sounds sweeter than the song of a nightingale, and sides of bacon are the very best ornaments of the cottage walls,' enthused a country squire in 1857. Conscientious landlords established village pig shows.

> In the West Riding [of Yorkshire] the competition in pigs was keener than in any other part of England. The villages had their little events and there was scarcely a town without an Agricultural Society, or at least a Pig and Poultry Show. At these shows there was often a row of 20 or 30 fat pigs, worth from £6 to £12 each, all as white as soap and water could make them, stretched on beds of clean straw, with wrappers of some kind to protect them from the sun or rain …
>
> Piggie is capitally cared for; on washing days, the family suds are saved for him; two or three times a week, during the short leisure of dinner-hour, he is walked out for a few minutes for exercise. Every week he is measured to see how much he has gained, and, when the show-day arrives, he travels to the field in a van; if he wins the prize, the owner is a hero, and his neighbours hold a festival in honour of the pig.

SAMUEL SIDNEY, *The Pig*, 1897

Fattest Pigs

Americans took up the competition for the fattest pig with enthusiasm. An English writer, Sanders Spencer, reported on this in his book *Pigs*, published in 1897. In view of the appalling obesity found at British pig shows, his disapproving tone is distinctly hypocritical.

Pig breeders in the States favoured those pigs which were considered to be the best lard and fat-meat-making machines ... This influence was also aided by the general craze of those American farmers, in whose life there was little opportunity to favour competition with their neighbours, or comparatively no other amusement or employment than hard work, to make their fat pigs the medium of speculation or gambling. Sweepstakes were started for the heaviest pigs in the various districts. When the weighing-in day arrived – you could scarcely call it judging – the majority of the farmers within many miles of the place of meeting would attend, and a real good day of it was made. The pride of place for the season amongst hog-raisers was not won without considerable outlay of food and attention spread over a year or two at least, as to have any chance of success the fat hog must have scaled at least 1,000 lbs, whilst 1,200 to 1,300 lbs hogs are recorded.

The Beginning of the End of the Fat Pig

After a visit to the Cattle Show of the Royal Agricultural Society of England in 1852, a clergyman was so upset by the fat pigs, that he wrote and published a remonstrance to the Society.

Being on a restorative visit to Brighton, I went, on Thursday, 13th ult. [of the previous month] to see the Cattle Show – I expected a day of unusual gratification and delight. But I am grieved to confess that those pleasurable enjoyments were far more than counterbalanced, by feeling – of the deepest pain, – of pitying disgust, – and of utter amazement.

My pain arose from witnessing animals unable to stand, and scarcely able to move or breathe, from the state of overwhelming and torturing obesity, to which they had been unnaturally forced.

The pitiable swine were so distorted by swollen obesity, that the shape of their heads (as swine) to except the extreme nostril circle, could not possibly be traced. Nor could one of the unhappy prize pigs, or of those exhibited to contest the prize, stand for one moment. And, if punished by being partially raised, to gratify the brutish curiosity of a few, they laid themselves down, or rather fell down, immediately, And it appears, that several died in their cart-conveyance to the scene of this cruel and unchristian exhibition.

THE REV. HENRY COLE

The Beauty of Fat Pigs

However unprofitable fat pigs became for farmers, however cruel their vast bulk may have been, they had a charm all of their own. The best description of their glorious size was written by the essayist, G.K. Chesterton (1874–1936).

To begin with, pigs are very beautiful animals. Those who think otherwise are those who do not look at anything with their own eyes, but only through other people's eyeglasses. The actual lines of a pig (I mean a really fat pig) are among the loveliest and most luxuriant in nature; the pig has the same great curves, swift and yet heavy, which we see in rushing water or in rolling cloud.

There is no point of view from which a really corpulent pig is not full of sumptuous and satisfying curves. You can examine the pig from the top of an omnibus, from the top of the Monument, from a balloon, or an airship; and as long as he is visible he will be beautiful. In short, he has that fuller, subtler, and more universal kind of shapeliness which the unthinking (gazing at pigs and distinguished journalists) mistake for a mere absence of shape. For fatness itself is a valuable quality. While it creates admiration in the onlookers, it creates modesty in the possessor.

PERFORMING PIGS, POINTER PIGS AND PET PIGS

Pigs are probably the most intelligent animals on the farm. In Britain a One Man and His Pig display team is a popular turn at agricultural shows. In America a pig that competed against dogs in obedience trials came first without any difficulty. Pigs have worked as drug detectors and even as dry-rot-sniffers.

One of the most famous porcine personalities was Slut, a New Forest sow, who was trained as a pointer to detect game. She used to come to a whistle and showed the greatest enthusiasm at the sight of a gun.

The same keen scenting ability has made pigs excellent truffle hunters in France and Italy. Even in Britain pigs have been used to dig up the gourmet fungi. Pigs were regularly used as plough animals in Minorca and in parts of Scotland.

These sagacious animals also show a surprising turn of speed and can be trained as race pigs. In the Highlands of Scotland, a widow used to back her pig to beat any pony on a course of her choosing. 'He had been trained over the course, and there was the pricking of his appetite to boot, and so the old lady won her money,' reports a writer of the 1870s.

Celebrity pigs also went into showbusiness. In the eighteenth century, a Learned Pig (we do not know his name) amused audiences with his ability to do maths, spell words and pick out cards. A few decades later, a similar

entertainer, known as Toby the Sapient Pig, had an equally illustrious career.

'This most extraordinary creature will Spell and Read, Cast Accounts, Play at Cards, Tell any Person what o'clock it is to a minute by their own watch; also tell the Age of Anyone in Company, and what is more Astonishing he will Discover a Person's Thoughts,' claimed Toby's trainer.

Barnum and Bailey's Greatest Show on Earth had a troupe of remarkable trained pigs, performing numerous difficult, clever and wonderful tricks. A poster shows one playing 'God Save the Queen' and the other 'Yankee Doodle' on xylophones.

Not only are pigs intelligent; they are affectionate and will occasionally fall hopelessly in love with human beings. I am pleased to say that some discerning humans treat these charming animals with reciprocal warmth. Good owners have even allowed devoted porkers into the bedroom and on the bed with them.

[34]

The First Learned Pig

Parson James Woodforde went to see the first learned pig at Norwich, when he was on tour round the provinces in 1785. The clever animal caused a stir. The poet William Cowper complained: 'I have a competitor for fame, not less formidable, in the Learned Pig. Alas! what is a tutor's popularity worth, in a world that can suffer a pig to eclipse his brightest glories?' Parson Woodforde, on the other hand, was impressed by the pig.

> After Dinner the Captain and myself, went and saw the learned Pigg at the rampant Horse in St Stephens – there was but a small Company there but soon got larger – We stayed there about an Hour – It was wonderful to see the sagacity of the Animal – It was a Boar Pigg, very thin, quite black with a magic Collar on his Neck. He would spell any word or Number from the Letters and Figures that were placed before him. Paid for seeing the Pigg one shilling.

Toby, a Later Sapient Pig

Toby, like showbusiness celebrities of today, wrote his autobiography – *The Life and Adventures of Toby the Sapient Pig, with his Opinions on Men and Manners, Written by Himself, Embellished with an elegant frontispiece descriptive of a Literary Pig Stye with the author in deep Study. Published and sold by Nicholas Hoare, Proprietor and Teacher of Toby.* In the book he describes his early struggles.

I was born in a place called Aversall, on the Duke of Bedford's demesnes. My father was an independent gentleman who roamed at large over his Grace's lands; and my mother a spinster in the service of a person whose name I have forgot … .On my natal day, the first of April 1816, the gentleman, who has since been my friend and preceptor, and to whom I owe every comfort I now enjoy, from the great care he has all along taken in the cultivation of my mind and manners, was travelling that road … From his bringing me up by hand in the way he did, and having no one to associate with but himself, I imbibed an affection for him, that will end only with my last breath … he never thrashed me but once … Whenever he set about giving me a lesson, day or night were alike to him in so doing; watching every movement of my mind with a solicitude indescribable, and a promptness of application never equalled by any of the learned teachers at either of our Universities ... By the time I was four months old, I could read tolerably well ... by the time I was six months old, he deemed it fit that I should make my first bow to an audience.

More about Toby

Toby boasted of his temperance and of his fans. 'A gentleman who one evening witnessed my performance, was so struck with it, that he wrote as follows.'

Whether heaven to brutes has imparted a mind
Is a query that moralists have not defined;
Perhaps it may rather arise from their pride
Than their reason, that reason to brutes they've denied.
Those, at least, who the Sapient Toby have seen,
To the latter opinion decidedly lean.
His symptoms of sense deep astonishment raise,
And elicit applause of wonder and praise.
But scarce can a doubt any longer remain,
The reason that Toby displays is so plain;
Here wisdom itself greater wisdom may find,
And no longer be vain of the rational mind.
Here the silken robed peer and the delicate belle,
Are unsullied by filth, unoffended by smell;
Toby turns all disdainful from deeds of offence,
For what would so blast his pretensions to sense?
Of the crowds who the Sapient Toby have seen,
Not one of them all disappointed have been.

Jemmy Hirst and His Pigs

Jemmy Hirst was a Yorkshire eccentric, who rode a bull out hunting, and used pigs as pointers. In 1880 a Martin Sis (probably a pseudonym) wrote a slim book with a lengthy title *The Life of Jemmy Hirst (King of Rawcliffe), Shewing what a Queer boy he was and how he chose to be a Tanner from Love to his Master's Daughter; then after her death how he became notorious as the Most Eccentric Man in England with particulars of his Outlandish dress, his riding on a Bull, Teaching Pigs to point at Game, Etc.; also a glance at his Triumphal Entry into London, and Reception at the Court of His Majesty King George II; with an account of Jemmy's Burial, when his remains were carried to the Grave by Eight Old Maids, preceded by an Aberdeen piper etc. etc.*

Jemmy was sent to a boarding school in Pontefract kept by a clergyman … Jemmy's great enjoyment about this time was in riding on the back of an old sow belonging to the parson. He used to tie a piece of twine to the ring in her snout, and call it his bridle; and a nail stuck in his shoe heel served for a spur. But, like most of her sex, the old sow was very wayward and obstinate; and many were the falls Jemmy got from her ladyship's back, and many a tussle he had with her before he succeeded in breaking her in. He had just got her to leap over a stick about a foot high, and was practising this novel equestrian feat one night after school hours, when who should come in to the yard, but the principal himself, bringing a horsewhip with him, with which he gave Jemmy two or three strokes on the shoulders …

Jemmy Hirst was partial to pigs, entertaining a higher opinion of their mental capacity than we generally hear expressed. So Jemmy Hirst chose for his pointers only smart active members of the Berkshire or Hampshire breeds … Jemmy took a number of sucking pigs – three, I believe – fresh from the pap then fed them by the hand, to the intent that they should watch their master's movements and obey him. Everybody knows that the natural propensity of the porcine race is to grunt. But grunting will not do in a pointer – stillness and stealthiness are essential requisites in a setter – so every time the neophytes grunted, chastisement ensued. The tutor got such command over his pigs that they would follow him anywhere; but the great difficult lay in teaching them to discriminate game; and to stand or sit still, pointing in their direction, whenever the pigs saw hares, rabbits, pheasants or partridges. Jemmy knew that pigs have even a finer nose than pointer dogs; the grand object was in getting them to discern what their master wanted. To accomplish this it became necessary to employ in conjunction with his pigs a pointer dog, and after much labour he succeeded so far as to make at least one of his porcine favourites to shoot over.

Slut, the Pointer Pig

Toomer, Gamekeeper to Sir Henry Mildmay, actually broke a Black Sow to find game, and to back and stand. The first step was to give her a name, and that of Slut (given in consequence of soiling herself in a Bog) she acknowledged in the course of the day, and never afterwards forgot. Within a fortnight she would find and point Partridges or Rabbits; she daily improved, and in a few weeks would retrieve Birds that had run as well as the best Pointer, nay, her Nose was superior to the best Pointer they ever possessed. She has sometimes stood a Jack-snipe when all the pointers had passed by it … In consequence of the Dogs not liking to hunt when she was with them (for they dropped their Sterns and showed symptoms of Jealousy) she did not very often accompany them … Her pace was mostly a Trot, was seldom known to Gallop, except when called to go out shooting; she would then come home off the Forest at full stretch .

THE REVEREND W.B. DANIEL c.1813

Carriage Pigs

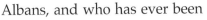

A Novelty was seen at St Albans, in October 1811, and which proves, that PIGS if managed with Address, are not of such a doltish Material, as admits of no Improvement. A Man, who holds a small Farm near St Albans, and who has ever been looked upon, as a most eccentric Being, made his Entree into the latter Place, in the following manner, viz. mounted on a small Car, which was actually drawn, by four large Hogs. He entered the Town at a brisk trot, amidst the Acclamations of Hundreds, who were soon drawn together, to witness this uncommon spectacle. After making the Tour of the Market-place three or four times, he came into the Wool Pack-yard, had his swinish Cattle regularly unharnessed, and taken into a Stable together, where they were regaled with a Trough full of Beans and Wash. They remained about two Hours, whilst he dispatched his Business as usual in the Market, when they were put to, and driven home again, Multitudes cheering him. This Man has only had these Animals under training six Months, and it is truly surprising, to what a high state of Tractability he has brought them. A Gentleman on the Spot, offered him Fifty pounds for the Concern as it stood, but it was indignantly refused.

THE REVEREND W.B. DANIEL c. 1813

On Pigs as Pets

The writer G.K. Chesterton may have been more prescient than he realised, when he wrote about pigs as pets. The advent of the mini-pig in the USA has made pet pigs more practical. And in North China there is a hairy pig, known as the Min pig (perhaps not unlike the now-extinct Cumberland curly-coated pig), which could possibly provide genes for the eventual poodle-pig.

We do not know what fascinating variations might happen in the pig if once the pig were a pet ... Types of Pig may also be differentiated; delicate shades of Pig may also be produced. A monstrous pig as big as a pony may perambulate the streets like a St Bernard without attracting attention. An elegant and unnaturally attenuated pig may have all the appearance of a greyhound. There may be little frisky, fighting pigs like Irish or Scotch terriers; there may be little pathetic pigs like King Charles spaniels ... Those interested in hairdressing might amuse themselves by arranging the bristles like those of a poodle. Those fascinated by the Celtic mystery of the Western Highlands might see if they could train the bristles to be a veil or curtain for the eye, like those of a Skye terrier; that sensitive and invisible Celtic spirit. With elaborate training one might have a sheep-pig instead of a sheep-dog, a lap-pig instead of a lap-dog. What is it that makes you look so incredulous?

A Clerical Pig

Probably the first recorded clerical pig was the one belonging to the vicar-poet Robert Herrick, best known for writing 'Gather Ye Rosebuds While Ye May'. Robert Stephen Hawker, another poetical parson, in imitation of either Herrick or St Anthony, also kept one. When his sister-in-law objected to it in her house, he would retort: 'He's as well behaved as any of your family'. Alas, neither poet put pigs into their poetry.

Robert Stephen Hawker was ordained priest in 1831, by the Bishop of Bath and Wells. He took his M.A. degree in 1836. He had a favourite rough pony which he rode, and a black pig of Berkshire breed, well cared for, washed, and curry-combed, which ran beside him when he went out for walks, and paid visits. Indeed, the pig followed him into ladies' drawing-rooms, not always to their

satisfaction. The pig was called Gyp, and was intelligent and obedient. If Mr Hawker saw that those whom he visited were annoyed at the intrusion of the pig, he would order it out; and the black creature slunk out of the door with its tail out of curl.

SABINE BARING-GOULD

[43]

A Legal Pig

Lord Gardenstone, a Scottish lawyer who would drink himself into a stupor at night then sparkle in the law court the following morning, was passionate about pigs. This account comes from *A Series of Original Portraits*, published in 1837.

Among the eccentricities of Lord Gardenstone was an attachment to the generation of pigs. He had reared one of these animals with so much affectionate care, that it followed him wherever he went like a dog. While it was little, he allowed it even to share his bed during the night. As it grew up, however, which it no doubt would do rapidly under such patronage, this was found inconvenient; and it was discarded from the bed, but permitted still to sleep in the apartment, where his lordship accommodated it with a couch composed of his own clothes, which he said kept it in a state of comfortable warmth …

My father called upon his lordship one morning, but he was not yet out of bed. He was shown into his bedroom, and in the dark, he stumbled over something which gave a terrible grunt. Upon which Lord Gardenstone said, 'It is just a bit sow, poor beast, and I laid my breeches on it to keep it warm all night'.

A Sea-going Pig

Captain Basil Hall, a Royal Naval captain in the first half of the nineteenth century, wrote an amusing account of a ship's mascot on his voyage out to China. One of the six sows taken for food was adopted by the crew and christened Jean. After her death, she was given a proper burial at sea, rather than being eaten.

In warm latitudes, the men generally take their meals on deck, and it was Jean's grand amusement, as well as business, to cruise along amongst the messes, poking her snout into every bread-bag. Occasionally, the sailors, to shew the extent of their regard, amused themselves by pouring a drop of grog down her throat. I never saw her fairly drunk, however, but twice; upon which occasions, as was to be expected, she acted pretty much like a human being in the same hoggish predicament.

On reaching the quarter-deck … I called out

[45]

'Jean! Jean!' and in a moment the delighted pig came prancing along. I felt that Jean now belonged more to the ship's company than to myself, and that there was a sort of obligation upon me neither to eat her nor to give her away.

After a time she became so excessively fat and lazy that it required many a call to get her to move. As she advanced in fatness, she lost altogether the power of walking, and expected the men to bring the good things of their tables to her, instead of allowing her to come for them. This was cheerfully done ...

Both her eyes were ringed up by huge bolsters of fat, which admitted only a slender chink of light between them. As she had long lost the power of locomotion, she generally lay flat on her side all day long, giving out a low sort of grunt for more food about once every hour. At this stage of her happiness, two of her legs only touched the deck, the others being rigged out horizontally; but as she became fatter and fatter, the upper pair of legs gradually formed an angle with the horizon, and eventually assumed the position of 45 degrees. The lower legs next began to leave the deck, as the rotundity of her corporation became greater, till, at length all four legs were erected towards the heavens, and it became a source of discussion amongst the curious as to which side she was actually lying upon.

At length poor dear Jean gave token of approaching dissolution; she could neither eat, nor drink, nor even grunt; and her breathing was like that of a broken bellows: in short she died!

A Pet Pig's Tomb

The most aristocratic pet pig was called Cupid. He fell in love, it is said, with the Earl of Edgecumbe and then became the faithful friend of the Countess. He followed her everywhere, came in for meals, and accompanied her on visits to London.

When this loyal and affectionate creature died, it was buried in a gold casket. A monument was erected to its memory by the Earl's son, Lord Valletort. The poet, Peter Pindar (real name Dr John Walcot) wrote this short piece to comfort the Countess.

A Consolatory Stanza

> O dry that tear, so round and big;
> Nor waste in sighs your precious wind!
> Death only takes a single Pig –
> Your Lord and Son are
>   still behind.

PIGS IN POETRY, PROSE AND ART

Pigs, who have suffered undeserved scorn at the pens of poets, have the distinction of appearing in one of the earliest epic poems, Homer's *Odyssey*. True, they appear only when the enchantress Circe turns sailors into swine, and as the supporting cast to Eumaeus, the swineherd who accompanies Odysseus home to his palace.

Homer, I am afraid, did not really do pigs justice. Nevertheless it is often in the early translations of the *Odyssey* that pigs first appear in English literature. They also make a brief appearance in Michael Drayton's poetic account of Noah's Ark.

Poets are mostly townies, who spend their time talking and drinking in low-life dives. Pigs, therefore, remain a rare subject for verse. Those few poets who have written about them sensitively are usually the country-dwellers, brought up in cottages with their own sty.

Alas, most poets, no doubt happy to sit down to roast pork with crackling, have nonetheless sneered at the living animal. So the pig-lover can turn his back on the works of Robbie Burns, James Thomson and George Orwell.

It was left to Robert Southey, undoubtedly the kindest if not the best of the Romantic poets, to pay proper honour to the pig. His poem, 'The Pig', is a turning point in porcine literature and marks the moment when this worthy animal became fit subject for verse.

As the romantic movement continued, animals began to creep into novels and essays, as well as verse. Writers like George Eliot, Charles Dickens and Mark Twain appreciated the beauty of pigs. Essayists like Leigh Hunt were inspired by their charm. Pigs also began to appear in paintings. When Thomas Gainsborough exhibited a painting of a girl and some pigs in 1782, it created quite a stir. Peter Pindar, a versifier of the day, suggested that the painter did the pig rather better than the girl, while a farmer who was shown it said, 'To be sure they be deadly like pigs, but there is one fault; nobody ever saw three pigs feeding together, but what one on 'um had a foot in the trough.'

It was George Morland, the hardest-working, deepest-drinking artist of them all, who painted pigs in all their glory over and over again. 'Pigs and asses were his chief favourites,' according to an early biographer.

Perhaps the new century will finally see proper homage paid to this noble animal. Were pigs to be portrayed in all their beauty, people might feel uneasy about the cruel way we treat them. We look down upon them, who are undeserving of our scorn; they look up to us, who are equally undeserving of their respect.

The First Poetic Porkers

The first appearance of pigs in literature is in the *Odyssey* which tells of the journey home of the hero Odysseus (or Ulysses) after the Trojan war ended. During his wanderings, he comes across a sorceress, the goddess Circe, who turns his followers into pigs. Odysseus persuades her to transform them back.

Instant her circling wand the Goddess waves
To hogs transforms 'em, and the Sty receives.
No more was seen the human form divine,
Head, face and members bristle into swine;
Still curst with sense, their mind remains alone,
And their own voice affrights them when they groan.
Meanwhile the Goddess in disdain bestows
The mast and acorn, brutal food! and strows
The fruits of cornel, as their feast, around;
Now prone, and grovelling on unsav'ry ground …

With that she parted: in her potent hand
She bore the virtue of the magic wand.
Then hast'ning to the styes set wide the door,
Urg'd forth, and drove the bristly herd before;
Unwieldy, out They rushed, with gen'ral cry,
Enormous beasts dishonest to the eye.
Now touch'd by counter-charms, they changed agen
And stand majestic, and recalled to men.

trans. ALEXANDER POPE

Philosophic Pigs in Love

Plutarch, the Roman philosopher and writer, was probably the first to maintain the pig's superiority over man. In an essay arguing that animals are reasonable beings, he reports a conversation between the enchantress Circe, Ulysses (the Roman name for Odysseus) and the enchanted pig, Gryllus. This is Gryllus' praise of pig love.

Sows ... are incited to copulation out of common affection; the female without the coynesses of women, or the practice of little frauds and fascinations, to inflame the lust of their mates; and the males, not with amorous rage and frenzy stimulated, and enforced to purchase the act of generation with expensive hire or servile assiduity, but enjoying their seasonable amours without deceit or purchase of the satisfaction of their venery. For Nature in the springtime, even as she puts forth the buds of plants, likewise awakens the desires of animals, but presently quenches them again, neither the female admitting the male nor the male attempting the female after conception.

Pigs in an Elizabethan Ark

Here is the pig in native English literature for the first time, appearing in Michael Drayton's charming poem, 'Noah's Flood'. I don't think the Elizabethan poet knew much about the life of a wild pig, but nonetheless he gives it six lines to itself!

When Noah sets ope the Ark and doth begin
To take his fraught, his mighty lading in
And now the beasts are walking from the wood,
As well of ravine, as that chew the cud …
The stately courser for his mare doth neigh,
And t'wards the new Ark guideth her the way;
The wreathed-horned ram his safety doth pursue,
And to the Ark ushers his gentle ewe;
The bristly boar, who with his snout up-ploughed
The spacious plains, and with his grunting loud,
Raised rattling echoes all the woods about,
Leaves his dark den, and having scented out
Noah's new-built Ark, in with his sow doth come,
And stye themselves up in a little room.

[53]

The Pig's Complaint

The first English poem from the pig's point of view, 'The Boar', was written by George Granville, a poet, playwright and politician, who lived from 1667 to 1735. Like Plutarch, Granville can see the pig's superiority to humankind.

A boar who had enjoyed a happy span
For many a year and fed on many a man,
Called to account, softening his savage eyes,
Thus suppliant pleads his cause before he dies;
'For what am I condemned? My crime's no more
To eat a man than yours to eat a boar.
We seek not you, but take what chance provides,
Nature and mere necessity our guides;
You murder us in sport, then dish us up
For drunken feats, a relish for the cup.
We lengthen not our meals; but you much feast;
Gorge till your bellies burst – pray who's the beast?
With your humanity you keep a fuss,
But are in truth worse brutes than all of us.'

Pigs and the Farmer's Boy

It is the poets from humble backgrounds like Robert Bloomfield (1766–1823), who do justice to the pig. Bloomfield wrote his first poem in a garret, and *The Farmer's Boy* sold 26,000 copies. Alas, Bloomfield died half blind, half mad and wholly poor. He describes pigs in the 'Autumn' section of his poem.

No more the fields with scattered grain supply
The restless wandering tenants of the sty;
From oak to oak they run with eager haste,
And wrangling share the first delicious taste
Of fallen acorns …
The trudging sow leads forth her numerous young,
Playful, and white, and clean, the briars among,
Till briars and thorns increasing, fence them round,
Where last year's mouldering leaves bestrew the ground,
And o'er their heads, loud lashed by furious squalls,
Bright from their cups the rattling treasure falls;
Hot, thirsty food; whence doubly sweet and cool
The welcome margin of some rush-grown pool,
The wild duck's lonely haunt, whose jealous eye
Guards every point; who sits, prepared to fly …
And as the bold intruders press around,
At once she starts, and rises with a bound;
With bristles raised the sudden noise they hear,
And ludicrously wild, and winged with fear,
The herd decamp with more than
     swinish speed,
And snorting dash through sedge, and
     rush and reed.

A Proper Pig Poem

Robert Southey was a better man than poet – kind to children, passionately fond of cats, always helpful and generous to struggling writers. 'This morning I have written a poem upon a Pig,' he wrote to his brother in 1799 having finished the poem, 'which will, I think, be the best of all my quaint pieces'.

> Jacob! I do not love to see thy nose
> Turned up in scornful curve at yonder pig.
> It would be well, my friend, if thou and I
> Had, like that pig, attained the perfectness
> Made reachable by Nature! why dislike
> The sow-born grunter? – He is obstinate,
> Thou answerest, ugly and the filthiest beast
> That banquets upon offal. Now I pray you
> Hear the pig's counsel.
>   Is he obstinate?
> We must not, Jacob, be deceived by words,
> By sophist sounds. A democratic beast,
> He knows that his unmerciful drivers seek
> Their profit, and not his. He hath not learnt
> That pigs were made for man, born to be brawn'd
> And baconized; that he must please to give
> Just what his gracious masters please to take;
> Perhaps his tusks, the weapons Nature gave
> For self-defence, the general privilege …
>
>   Jacob look at him!
> Those eyes have taught the lover flattery.
> His face – nay, Jacob, Jacob! were it fair
> To judge a lady in her dishabille?

Fancy it drest, and with saltpetre rouged.
Behold his tail, my friend; with curls like that
The wanton hop marries her stately spouse;
So crisp in beauty Amoretta's hair
Rings round her lover's soul the chains of love.
And what is beauty but the aptitude
Of parts harmonious? give thy fancy scope,
And thou wilt find that no imagined change
Can beautify this beast. Place at his end
The starry glories of the peacock's pride;
Give him the swan's white breast for his horn-hoofs;
Shape such a foot and ankle as the waves
Crowded in eager rivalry to kiss,
When Venus from the enamoured
        sea arose; –
Jacob, thou canst but make a
        monster of him;
All alteration man could think
        would mar
His pig-perfection ...

Pigs Through The Year

Another pig-loving poet was John Clare (1793–1864), the uneducated son of a farm labourer but far more talented than Bloomfield. He wrote in a Northamptonshire dialect, which sometimes makes his poems difficult to understand. Here is his account of pigs through the year.

January   While whining hogs wi hungry roar
                   Crowd around the kitchen door
                   Or when their scanty meal is done
                   Creep in the straw the cold to shun.

February   The gladdend swine bolt from the sty
                   And round the yard in freedom run
                   Or stretching in their slumbers lye
                   Beside the cottage in the sun

October   The free horse rustling through the stubble land
                   And bawling herd boy with his motley band
                   Of hogs and sheep and cows who feed their fill
                   O'er cleard fields rambling where so ere they will.

[58]

On the Graces and Anxieties of Pig-driving

Pigs snuffled their way into the essays of Leigh Hunt, the writer and critic who was once imprisoned in a Surrey gaol for writing rude things about the Prince Regent. (He decorated his cell with a trellis of roses and played battledore in it.) Hunt had the gift of recognising and enjoying the charm of everyday things, including pig driving.

The other day we happened to be among a set of spectators who could not help stopping to admire the patience and address with which a pig-driver huddled and cherished onward his drove of unaccomodating *élèves* down a street in the suburbs. To see that *hand* with which he did it! How hovering, yet firm, how encouraging, yet compelling; how indicative of the space to each side of him, and yet of the line before him; how general, how particular, how perfect! No barber's could quiver about a head with more lightness of apprehension; no cook's pat up and proportion the side of a pasty with a more final eye ...

The pigs did not exult, but they knew their king. Unwilling was their subjection, but, 'more in sorrow than in anger' ... They did not see why they should proceed, but they felt themselves bound to do so; forced, onwards, irresistibly impelled by fate and Jenkins. They squeaked and grunted as in ordinary; they sidled, they shuffled, they half stopped; they turned an eye to all the little outlets of escape; but in vain. There they stuck (for their very progress was a sort of sticking), charmed into the centre of his sphere of action, laying their heads together, but to no purpose; looking all as if they were shrugging their shoulder, and eschewing the tip-end of the whip of office. Much eye had they to their left leg; shrewd backward glances; not a little anticipative squeak and sudden rush of avoidance. It was a superfluous clutter, and they felt it; but a pig finds it more difficult than any other animal to accommodate himself to circumstances. Being out of his pale, he is in the highest state of wonderment and inaptitude. He is sluggish, obstinate, opinionate, not very social; has no desire of seeing foreign parts. Judge by this of the talents of his driver.

The Pig's Revenge

Oliver Wendell Holmes (1809–1894) wrote a poem in which the pig comes back from the dead to get his revenge, entitled 'The Spectre'.

> Back flew the bolt, up rose the latch,
> And open swung the door,
> And little mincing feet were heard
> Pat, pat along the floor.
>
> 'Now wake, now wake, thou butcher man!
> What makes thy cheek so pale?
> Take hold! take hold! thou dost not fear
> To clasp a spectre's tail?'
>
> Untwisted every winding coil;
> The shuddering wretch took hold,
> All like an icicle it seemed
> So tapering and so cold.
>
> And open, open swung the door,
> And, fleeter than the wind,
> The shadowing spectre
>   swept before,
> The butcher trailed behind.
>
> Straight, straight towards
>   thatoaken beam,
> A trampled pathway ran;
> A ghastly shape was swinging
>   there, –
> It was the butcher man.

[61]

The Cottage Pig

The Victorian English novelist, George Eliot, described the happy lot of the cottager's pig. While pigs in the big farms were losing their freedom to ramble round the farmyard, the cottage pig was still relatively free. His status was high, too, among English farm workers. In *Scenes from Clerical Life*, George Eliot describes a particularly fortunate animal.

Such was Dame Fripp, whom Mr Filfil (the clergyman), riding leisurely in top-boots and spurs from doing duty at Knebley one warm Sunday afternoon, observed sitting in the dry ditch near her cottage, and by her side a large pig, who, with that ease and confidence belonging to perfect friendship, was lying with his head in her lap, and making no effort to play the agreeable beyond an occasional grunt.

'Why, Mrs Fripp,' said the Vicar, 'I didn't know you had such a fine pig. You'll have some rare flitches at Christmas!'

'Eh, God forbid! My son gev him me two 'ear ago, an' he's been company to me iver sin'. I couldn't find i' my heart to part wi'm, if I niver knowed the taste o' bacon-fat again.'

'Why, he'll eat his head off, and yours too. How can you go on keeping a pig, and making nothing by him?'

'O, he picks a bit hisself wi' rooting', and I dooant mind doing wi'out to gi' him summat. A bit o' coompany's meat an' drink too, and' he followers me about, and grunts when I spake to'm, just like a Christian.'

Mark Twain on Hogs

The American writer Mark Twain had a natural feeling for pigs and his descriptions of them outdo those of any other novelist including George Eliot and Charles Dickens (whose description of American pigs is in Chapter One). Here are two passages from *Huckleberry Finn*.

There warn't anybody at the church, except maybe a hog or two, for there warn't any lock on the door, and hogs likes puncheon floor in summer-time because it's cool. If you notice, most folks don't go to church only when they've got to; but a hog is different …

All the streets and lanes was just mud, they warn't nothing else *but* mud – mud as black as tar and nigh about a foot deep in some places; and two or three inches deep in *all* the places. The hogs loafed and grunted around, everywheres. You'd see a muddy sow and a litter of pigs come lazying along the street and whollop herself right down in the way where folks had to walk around her, and she'd stretch out, and shut her eyes, and wave her ears, whilst the pigs was milking her, and look as happy as if she was on salary.

By kind permission of Iona Antiques, London

PROPHETIC PIGS, ENCHANTED PIGS AND HOLY PIGS

According to legend, pigs were once god-like creatures of power and might. Monstrous and fiercesome boars, like the one that killed Adonis, play a part in Greek myths. And pigs appear at a crucial moment in the voyage of Aeneas, founder of Rome.

The ancient Celts, the inhabitants of Northern Europe before the Romans, saw animals as symbols of power and influence, pigs included. There was even a pig-god, Moccus. In Ireland and in Wales, the last Celtic strongholds, myths and legends about pigs lingered on into medieval times. A pig was the familiar companion of Merlin the wizard, playing the same role as black cats do to witches. Thus pigs are associated with some of his prophecies.

The greatest of all the magical pigs, however, was Gullinbursti, or 'golden-bristled', from the pantheon of Norse gods. The radiant bristles of this boar represented both the rays of the sun and the golden grain of harvest. It was he who first taught mankind how to plough.

The God Frey was given Gullinbursti by the dwarfs. He rode him astride or harnessed him to a golden chariot. In some legends Gulllinbursti has a female counterpart, his sister, a sow called Hildisvin, who belongs to Freya, goddess of beauty.

There are legendary Christian pigs too. Pigs helped St Frideswide, patron saint of Oxford, to escape from Prince Algar of Mercia. She hid in their sty in

order to save her virginity. Irish saints like Brigid (who in her youth had worked as a swineherd) saved wild boars from the huntsmen.

The most famous pig-loving saint is St Anthony, a hermit saint in Egypt, who kept a pet pig. There is a story that Anthony was once asked to heal a prince in Barcelona, but he simultaneously heard of a piglet in distress. The saint hurried off to help the little porker, only attending the prince after he had restored the piglet to health. The smallest pig in the litter, the runt, is known as the Tantony pig, in his honour!

It is from the Norsemen that we get the winter festival of Yule, now christianised into Christmas. In honour of Frey, and golden Gullinbursti, boar meat was eaten during the feast and the boar's head was brought to the table with special ceremony.

Today, the turkey has taken the pig's place on the Christmas table but the boar's head ceremony still lingers on in ancient institutions. A special carol, sung yearly, is the only relic of those far-off days, when pigs accompanied the gods or were even gods themselves.

A Roman Prophetic Pig

A pig played its part in the foundation of the Roman state. In the *Aeneid*, the poet Virgil tells how a white sow shows Aeneas where the city of Rome will be built. Aeneas, a shockingly callous hero, responds by promptly sacrificing the whole porcine family to the goddess Juno.

> Fear not! the war shall end in lasting peace,
> And all the rage of haughty Juno cease.
> And that this nightly vision may not seem
> Th' effect of fancy, or an idle dream
> A sow beneath an oak shall lie along,
> All white herself, and white her thirty young.
> When thirty rolling years have run their race,
> Thy son Ascanius, on this empty space,
> Shall build a royal town …
>
> Now on the shore the fatal swine is found.
> Wondrous to tell! – She lay along the ground:
> Her well-fed offspring at her udders hung;
> She white herself, and white her thirty young.
> Aeneas takes the mother and her brood
> And all on Juno's altars are bestowed.

trans. JOHN DRYDEN

The Druidical Pig

Magic pigs abound in Celtic legends and sometimes their death brings disaster. The story of the Children of Turenn, adapted from P.W. Joyce's *Old Celtic Romances*, concerns three brothers, Ur, Urcar and Brian, whose adventures end in their death. Their downfall begins with the killing of a pig. Alas for them, it is a magic pig, none other than Kian, a faery warrior.

As soon as Kian saw these three brothers, he looked round, and seeing near him a herd of swine, he struck himself with a golden druidical wand, and changed himself into a pig; and he quickly joined the herd...

When the brothers had come near, the druidical pig fell out from the herd, and made towards a thick grove that grew hard by; but Brian was there before him, and drove his spear through his chest.

The pig screamed and said, 'You have done an ill deed to

cast your spear to me, for you know well who I am'.

'Your voice, methinks, is the voice of a man,' said Brian; 'but I know not who you are'.

And the pig answered, 'I am Kian, the son of Canta; and now I ask you to give me quarter'.

Ur and Urcar said, 'We will give you quarter indeed, and we are sorry for what has happened to you'. But Brian, on the other hand, said, 'I swear by the gods of the air, that if your life returned to you seven times, I would take it from you seven times.'

'Then,' said Kian, 'as you will not grant me quarter, allow me first to return to my own shape'.

'That we will grant you,' said Brian; 'for I often feel it easier to kill a man than to kill a pig'.

Kian accordingly took his own shape; and then he said, 'You indeed, ye sons of Turenn, are now about to slay me; but even so, I have outwitted you. For if you had slain me in the shape of a pig, you would have to pay only the eric-fine for a pig; whereas now that I am in my own shape, you shall pay the full fine for a man'.'You shall not be slain with the weapons of a warrior,' said Brian; and so saying, he and his brothers laid aside their arms, and smote him fiercely with the round stones of the earth. They then buried him a man's height in the earth.

Then the sons of Turenn prepared to go forward after Luga of the Long Arms to the battle. But as they were leaving the grave, they thought they heard a faint muffled voice coming up from the ground beneath their feet:

> 'The blood you have spilled,
> The hero you've killed,
> Shall follow your steps till your doom be fulfilled.'

The Voyage of Maeldune

The Celtic equivalent of the *Aeneid* or the *Odyssey* was the *Voyage of Maeldune*, in which the hero makes a boat out of three skins and sets off on a magic voyage. All kinds of wondrous events befall him, including an encounter with fiery pigs.

> And they came to another island … and in that island there were a great many fruit trees, having large golden apples upon them. And there were beasts like pigs, short and fiery, under those trees, and they used to go to the trees and to strike them with their hind legs till the apples would fall from them, and then they would feed upon them. And from morning to the setting of the sun those beasts did not show themselves at all, but they used to be stopping in caves of the ground … It was a fiery country, and the beasts used to throw out heat into the ground that was over them … And with the brightness of the morning the birds went from the island, swimming out to sea; and with that the fiery beasts began putting their heads out of the caves, and they were eating the apples till the setting of the sun. And when they would go back into the caves, the birds used to come and to be eating the apples.

trans. L<small>ADY</small> G<small>REGORY</small>

The Discovery of the Spa at Bath

The hot springs of the famous city of Bath, in the west of England, were first enjoyed by pigs in the keeping of Prince Baldred, then a swineherd. His statue can still be seen in the King's Bath in that city. Sadly, there are no statues to the pigs, to whom the credit of the discovery should really go.

Baldred, eldest son of Lord Hudibras, then King of Britain, it is said, having spent eleven years at Athens in study, came home leprous and was in consequence confined to prevent infection. Having effected his escape, however, he entered into service at Learwick, a small village, three miles from Bath, where his business was to take care of pigs. While at his usual employment one morning, part of the drove of swine, as if seized with a frenzy, ran down the side of the hill into an elder-moor, till they reached the spot of ground where the hot springs of Bath now boil up, and from thence returned, covered with black mud. The prince, being of a thoughtful turn ... observed, that after a while they became whole and smooth from their scabs and eruptions by often wallowing in this mud ... Upon this he considered within himself why he should not receive the same benefit by the like means. He tried the experiment with success, finding himself cured of his leprosy.

WILLIAM YOUATT

Prophecy to a Pig

Merlin the enchanter, the adviser to King Arthur of Britain, was often accompanied by a pig. In the Black Book of Carmarthen, (fifty-four folios in four different handwritings, compiled sometime between 1154 and 1189) is found a mysterious prophetic poem in Welsh addressed to this animal. Normally, Merlin's companion was a black pig, but in this version it seems to have been a spotted one, perhaps an early ancestor of the Gloucester Old Spot!

Listen, O little pig! thou happy little pig!
Bury not thy snout on the top of the mountain;
Burrow in a secluded place in the woods,
For fear of the hunting dogs of Rydderch, the champion of the faith.
And I will prognosticate, and it will be true ...

Listen, O little pig! hear thou now:
When the men of Gwynedd lay down their great work,
Blades will be in hands, horns will be sounded,
Armour will be broken before sharp lances.
And I will predict that two rightful princes
Will produce peace from heaven to earth …

Listen, O little pig! are not the buds of thorns
Very green, the mountain beautiful, and beautiful the earth?
And I will predict the battle of Coed Llwyvein,
And ruddy biers from the attack of Owein,
When stewards shall make short disputes,
And there will be perjury and treachery amongst the children of the land …

Listen, O little pig! thou little speckled
    one!
Listen to the voice of the sea birds,
    great is their energy!
I was told by a seagull that had
    come from afar,
That strange sovereigns will
    make their appearance;
Gwyddyl, and Brython, and
    Romani
Will create discord and
    confusion,
And in the name of the gods
    will come into it,
And vigorously fight on both
    banks of the Tywi.

A Disciple Pig

The Irish Celtic saints seem to have had a special tenderness towards animals. St Kiaran of Saigher, predecessor of St Patrick, worked many pig miracles: burning pig thieves, raising a pig from the dead and miraculously supplying a sow with twelve piglets when needed. This extract from the Life of St Kieran comes from a Gaelic manuscript, first translated in 1854.

And Kiaran came to the resolution of residing in that place as an eremite [hermit], for it was entirely surrounded with dense woods at that time: he commenced to construct temporary little cells, he next built a monastery, and afterwards a city ... When Kiaran came first there he sat under the shelter of a tree, and a very furious wild boar started up from the other side of the same tree, and when it saw Kiaran it fled; however it returned and became submissive to Kiaran, being tamed by God. That boar was the first disciple and monk that Kiaran had in that place. It was accustomed to go to the wood and gnaw twigs and straw to assist to construct the cell.

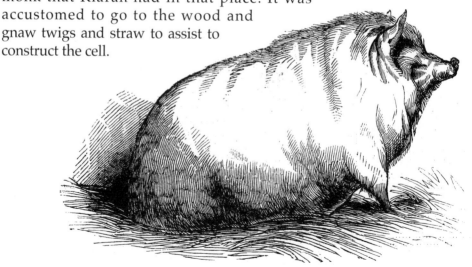

St Kevin and the Wild Boar

St Kevin was one of the most passionate animal lovers of all Irish saints. His monks wanted to level the mountains round Glendalough to make pastureland, but he refused to do so, saying it would disturb the wild creatures. Like St Brigid, he saved a wild boar from the huntsmen. Helen Waddell recounts the tale in her charming book, *Beasts and Saints.*

Then St Kevin commended his monastery to trusty men, and gave to each monk his charge. And himself went out alone to the head of the glen ... And the wild things of the mountains and the woods came and kept him company, and would drink water, like domestic creatures, from his hands ... After seven years, St Kevin built himself a little oratory of osiers, on the northern margin of the lake, where he might make his daily prayer to God ... There came a day when the huntsman of the King of Leinster, Brandubh son of Eochaid ... came down after his hounds into the glen, following a boar: and the boar made into St Kevin's oratory, but the hounds did not go in, but lay on their chests outside, before the gate. And there was St Kevin praying under a tree, and a crowd of birds perched on his shoulders and his hands, and flitting about him, singing to the saint of God. The huntsman looked; and dumbfounded he took his way back with his hounds, and for the sake of the holy solitary's blessing, let the boar go free. He told the marvel that he had seen to the King and to all of them.

The Temptations of St Anthony

Goblins came, on mischief bent,
To St Anthony in Lent.

'Come, ye goblins, small and big
We will kill the hermit's pig.

'While the good monk minds his book,
We the hams will cure and cook.

'While he goes down on his knees,
We will fry the sausages.

'While he David's psalms doth sing,
We will all to table bring.'

On his knees went Anthony
To those imps of Barbary.

'Good, kind goblins, spare his life,
He to me is child and wife.

'He indeed is good and mild
As 'twere any chrisom child.

'He is my felicity,
Spare, oh spare my pig to me!'

But the pig they did not spare,
Did not heed the hermit's prayer.

They the hams did cure and cook,
Still the good Saint read his book.

When they fried the sausages,
Still he rose not from his knees.

They did all to table bring,
He for grace the psalms did sing.

All at once the morning broke
From his dream the monk awoke.

There in the kind light of day
Was the little pig at play.

R.L GALES *fl. 1927*

The Swine of the Gods

The pig retained some of its mystery in Ireland right up to the beginning of this century. The poet W.B. Yeats collected this tale in 1902 for a book, *The Celtic Twilight*. The Connaught Fenians whom he mentions, were the equivalent of today's Provisional IRA.

A few years ago a friend of mine told me of something that happened to him when he was a young man and out drilling with some Connaught Fenians … They left the car and went further up the hill with their rifles, and drilled for a while. As they were coming down again they saw a very thin, long-legged pig of the old Irish sort, and the pig began to follow them. One of them cried out as a joke that it was a fairy pig, and they all began to run to keep up the joke. The pig ran too, and presently, how nobody knew, this mock terror became real terror, and they ran for their lives. When they got to the car they made the horse gallop as fast as possible, but the pig still followed. Then one of them put up his rifle to fire, but when he looked along the barrel he could see nothing. Presently they turned a corner and came to a village. They told the people of the village what had happened, and the people of the village took pitchforks and spades and the like, and went along the road with them to drive the pig away. When they turned the corner they could not find anything.

The Boar's Head Carol

One of the few surviving relic of the days when pigs walked with gods is this carol. It is still sung every year at Queen's College Oxford, and at some American universities. A similar relic is the custom in the Southern United States of eating a slice of boar head, called a jog jowl, on New Year's Day. It is supposed to bring luck in the coming year.

The boar's head in hands I bring,
With garlands gay and birds
    singing!
I pray you all, help me to
    sing,
Quis estis in convivio!
[Who are at this banquet.]

The boar's head I understand,
Is chief service in all this land!
Wheresoever it may be found,
Servitur cum sinapio!
[It is served with mustard.]

The boar's head I dare well say,
Anon after the twelfth day,
He takes his leave and goes away.
Exiuit tunc de patria!
[He went out from his native country.]

Acknowledgements

I have tried to obtain permission from copyright holders to reproduce the quotations in this book but there are some I could not trace. The publishers will be happy to rectify any omissions in future editions. I should like to thank the following for permission to reprint:

Darton Longman Todd, William B. Eerdmans Publishing Co., Constable Publishers and Mary Martin for an extract from *Beasts and Saints* by Helen Waddell, published in the UK and copyright 1995 by Darton, Longman and Todd, Ltd. and used by permission of the publishers, and published in North America by William B. Eerdmans Publishing Co.; Random House UK and Lucinda Lambton for an extract from *Beastly Buildings* by Lucinda Lambton, originally published by Jonathan Cape; A.P. Watt, on behalf of The Royal Literary Fund, for two extracts from *On Pigs as Pets*, in *The Uses of Diversity* by G.K. Chesterton; Random House UK and A.P. Watt on behalf of the Trustees of the Wodehouse Estate, and Random House UK for an extract from *Blandings Castle* by P. G. Wodehouse, published by Hutchinson; Colin Smythe Ltd. on behalf of Anne de Winton and Catherine Kennedy for an extract from *A Book of Saints and Wonders* by Lady Gregory; A.P. Watt on behalf of Michael Yeats and Simon and Schuster for an extract from 'Swine of the Gods' from *Celtic Twilight* by W.B. Yeats, in *Mythologies* by William Butler Yeats. Copyright © 1959 Mrs W.B. Yeats.

Picture credits

P. 8, *Cottage Hospitality* Collins, Haworth Art Gallery, Accrington, Lancs/Bridgeman Art Library; p.20, *A Prize Berkshire Sow Outside a Brick Sty*, Heath, Knowle/Iona Antiques, London; p. 32, *A Unappreciative Audience* Weekes/Fine Art Photographs; p. 48, *Farmyard Scene* Herring, Phillips, The International Fine Art Auctioneers/Bridgeman Art Library; p.64, *A Tamworth Cross with her Piglets*, unknown artist/Iona Antiques, London; Back cover painting of a Gloucester Old Spot Pig by J Miles © Gloucester Folk Museum (Gloucester City Council), 99–103 Westgate Street, Gloucester GL1 2PG, open Mon-Sat 10–5, and Sun (July–Sept only) 10–4.

While every attempt has been made to trace the copyright holders, this has not always been possible. Any omissions will be rectified in future reprints.